What R
Haiku for

"If you want a guidebook to finding your heart. . . . Skyler's book is that which you seek. She is an inspiration to us all. A Warrior Woman."

Janette Leclerc-Law

~

"How beautiful her writing is—so filled with truth, gentle yet profound wisdom, humility, love and the sacred non-dual teachings. What an honor to read her writing; she continues to have so much to teach and share and leads us through inspiring example. She is incredible and my absolute role model."

Adriane E Burkhart

~

"My deep gratitude for the immeasurable channeling of deep wisdom in her haiku. There's a blaze of light in every word—the broken and the holy. I think they are brilliant. Pure Tao."

Mary Guenther

~

"A fine treasure!"

Camilla England

~

"The author discovers and documents life's most naked moments with both exquisite grace and bracing candor. To read a haiku is to catch up to existence, if for only a moment."

Alexandra Richardson

"Writing Haiku gifts this artist with a golden pen, a sharp quick tongue and a sense of adventure into the depth of every day life lessons. With her focus on the path, the way, her dance of written wit and humor entertain and delight the reader in every direction. The center of the cyclone in this book is a safety zone to work through any catharsis as though touched by grace and compassion."

Lily Komalta Helmer

~

"Haiku is my favorite kind of poetry because it's simple. Skyler can write haiku, simple in form, but deep, thoughtful, and profoundly moving. Every one I've read has given me a moment's pause for reflection."

Sheryl Christmas

~

"Skyler writes from her heart ~ deep, sweet, real. She conveys many feelings in few words. I love her writing."

Louisa Gonyou

~

"Skyler's haiku will fill your heart with beauty, depth, tenderness, and strength. She meets our human struggles with compassion, lightness of touch, and grace."

Renee Beck

Haiku for the Hungry Heart

Other Books
by Skyler Darshini Freimann

One with the Sofa: A Taoist Guide for the Physically Challenged. Parker, Colorado: Outskirts Press, 2013.

Ring of Dreams by Skyler Rubin Posner aka Skyler Darshini Freimann). San Francisco, California: A California Living Book, 1979.

Heading for Home, Poems Along the Way. Portland, Oregon: Darshini Arts Press, 2018

Haiku for the Hungry Heart

by
Skyler Darshini Freimann

 Darshini Arts Press

Darshini Arts Press
Portland, Oregon
skypye38@gmail.com

Printed in the United States of America

ISBN-13: 978-1723492747
ISBN-10: 1723492744

Prepared for publication by Jerri-Jo Idarius of Creation Designs.
Preface by Allanya Guenther
Introduction by Frank Sanje Elliott

Dedication

For Allanya
with infinite love and gratitude

Table of Contents

Preface

Skyler Darshini Freimann is the most remarkable person I have ever known, both as a human being and as an endlessly creative artist. Her focus has always included exploration of the Divine that lives within us all. Her first major work addressing this topic was her book, "Ring of Dreams," built upon many hours attending and photographing boxing matches in the San Francisco Bay Area. The book is in the form of a Passion Play, matching biblical verses to drama in the ring. Her photographs are stunning.

The next to follow was "One with the Sofa: A Taoist Guide for the Physically Challenged." Again, using her background in art and photography, Skyler created photos with texts to deepen the meaning of her narrative: that we can be free of our physical and mental suffering and experience the joy of spirit. Through her unique and quirky approach, she assuages the challenges of those suffering from serious health problems, including her own.

Skyler knew from an early age that ART SAVES LIVES. She knew, because art has saved her life in a seriously dysfunctional family growing up. It saved her life each time a health crisis has descended like a sledgehammer on her body. It has given her a reason to live, to embrace life in it's fullness of love, laughter, spiritual focus and relationships; which are so much more important than the state of our bodies.

I hope you will join me in embracing Skyler's latest spiritual journey. Lose yourself, then find yourself, in this deeply spiritual guide to happiness and peace of mind.

Allanya Guenther

Introduction

It is with great honor and joy that I am asked to write a forward to Skyler Darshini Freimann's newest book, "HAIKU FOR THE HUNGRY HEART". In this inspiring book, Darshini has shown us the depths of her deepest inner longings and loves, as well as her fears and concerns. Weaving in and out of her chapters: Mindfulness, Life, Suffering, Ego/Mind, Spiritual Practice, Whimsy, Transformation, Spirit/God, Love, one finds the full range of her philosophical and emotional responses to a life which has been very challenging.

Her Haiku, while adhering strictly to the traditional 5-7-5 syllable tradition of Japanese Haiku, emanate her freedom of traditional bonds and beliefs. One senses a lifetime of struggle with physical and emotional pain which, while being devastating, shows victory of mind over negativity and obscurations. She soars like an eagle showing no signs of fear of death. The egoic self clinging, which describes most other people's approach to the culmination of life, is totally absent, replaced with the strong belief she has in her connection to all other life forms and not limited to this life only. This oneness of connection to all other beings cuts through time and space to an eternal communication with the universe.

Born in 1938 to parents in the Foreign Service, she experienced life in Columbia, Mexico, Italy, Canada, Hungary, Switzerland and Germany, until college age. She became a Catholic as a teen, and by the time she was 20, she was initiated into Vedanta, the mystical teachings of Hinduism, and given the name Darshini which means, among other things, "bringer of light." Even as a small child she experienced beings of light who brought her love and nurturing through a difficult childhood.

Skyler also showed ability in art and early in life became a prize winning photographer, which culminated in her first book, "Ring of Dreams", composed of black and white photos of professional boxers accompanied by quotes from the Bible.

Her second book, "One with the Sofa, a Taoist Guide for the Physically Challenged", is "an integration of words and pictures that play off each other in a way that could be described as a contemporary contribution to traditional Taoism".

Her next book "Heading for Home" is a collection of poems reflecting Darshini's mind and body approaching the culmination of life. It is inspiring, humorous, and an affirmation of her connection to universal qualities of compassion, love and light. It is illustrated by many of her black and white mandala line drawings, including those symbolizing balance, transformation and unity. All of her books are available at amazon.com, although "Ring of Dreams" was published under the name Skyler Rubin Posner. It is currently out of print but remains available not only on amazon.com, but other web sites as well.

Darshini received her M. A. in Transpersonal Counseling from John F. Kennedy University in Oakland California, and then moved to Portland, Oregon where, as a Licensed Professional Counselor, she developed a private practice specializing in counseling with a spiritual emphasis. The presence of Divine Light, or Spirit, has become a continuous state of being for her. She lives in heightened awareness of Oneness; both a joyful and indescribable journey.

Frank Sanje Elliott
Artist, Musician, Teacher

One

Mindfulness

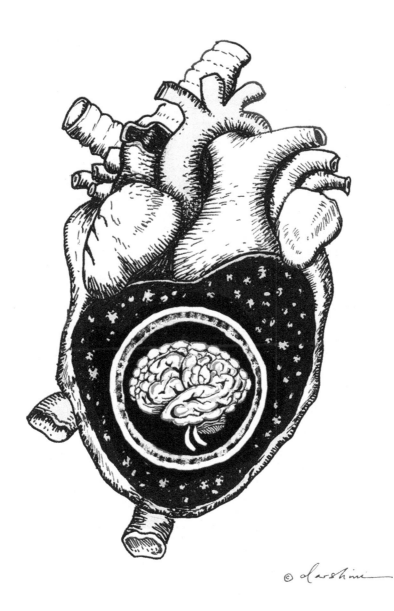

© Darshini

1

Beliefs prevent us
from believing in nothing
which is everything.

2

In full mindfulness
I embrace Truth beyond truth
and I beyond i.

3

Even with my feet
upon this earth, my home has
always been elsewhere.

4

When we feel the joy
of the miraculous, we
know we have come home.

5

The burning beauty
of galaxies seen tonight
tremble with secrets.

6

Toxic recluse bite.
Deadly bouquet of poison.
Pray for the spider.

7

Life's purpose is to
accept duality: As
Hitler, so the saint.

8

Knowing ourselves makes
us strong. Accepting ourselves –
unconquerable.

9

The wise look for truth
and find it in everything
and every no-thing.

10

When we're scared to try
and we try anyway, we
become a hero.

11

Take on the challenge
of spiritual life. Meet your
divine self within.

12

Allow your actions
to reflect your basic kind
and loving nature.

13

This morning I was
awakened by light. I am
beginning to see.

14

The real you is much
too big to just be you. You
are the all in All

15

Yes, you are divine.
Just look, my darling, and you
will see perfection.

16

Everything comes from
nothing. All beginnings come
from our emptiness.

17

Knowing that I am
not the doer, nor are you,
gives me peace of mind.

18

Although the movie
shows flooding rain and raging rivers,
the screen stays dry.

19

It is only our
aversions that hurt. Life in
itself is neutral.

20

We talk, hoping to
heal our hearts. Instead we need
to surrender them.

21

Others are only
you in so many mirrors;
sparks from the same flame.

22

The people who drive
us crazy are our greatest
guides and teachers.

23

No longer trying to
be an expert, good student
has become my goal.

24

If we call troubles
lessons, we'll become wiser
and strong as the earth.

25

When your thoughts become
meaningless, emptiness will
become your teacher.

26

The only thing to
take from any event is
what we learn from it.

27

Falling down is part
of living. Getting back up
makes life worth living.

28

The basis of life
is uncertainty. Peace of
mind is acceptance.

Two

Life

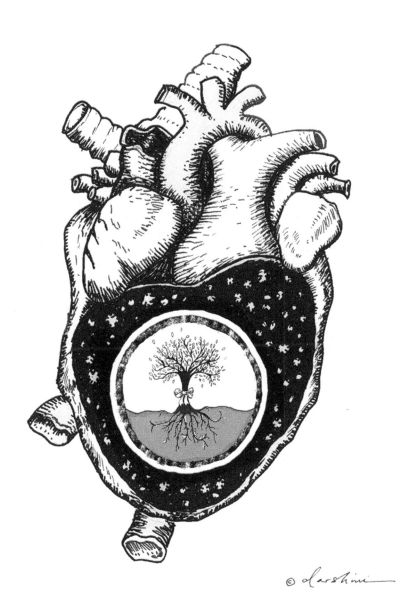

29

Be still. Let life flow.
Trust that whatever happens
is always perfect.

30

Middle of the night.
A train whistles. I am warm.
Sweet blessings abound.

31

Nothing to do. No
where to go. Nothing to grasp.
No one to do it.

32

Take my hand and I
will take yours. We will get through
this life together.

33

Today I am sad.
Tomorrow I am happy.
Feelings are like clouds.

34

I wear a coat of
flesh and fat and bones. But they
are not the real me.

35

We have descended
into human form and some
day we will rise up.

36

I have no practice
or faith. I live by letting
living happen.

37

How I respond is
more important than what is
happening to me.

38

Life does not need to
be accomplished. It needs to
be experienced.

39

Every new day is
an opportunity to
live with compassion.

40

If your belief is
just another thought, then you
might as well relax.

41

If we can't get out
of prison, we can choose to
share our meager meal.

42

All the lessons I
need to learn are written in
this present moment.

43

May I meet this night
fully. May I meet morning
as a precious friend.

44

Expectation means
being frustrated by God's
perfect authorship.

45

So, too, our lives play
out upon the movie screen
of divine dreaming.

46

When the body sleeps
we are sometimes more awake
than when we're awake.

47

When the day is done
and I have given my best
I need nothing else.

48

Cozy in my home.
Too many are without shelter
while I watch TV.

49

Attached to beliefs
Leaves us without the space to
believe in nothing.

50

If you think you can
or can't, you're right. You are the
mistress of your life.

51

Dawn, when all is still,
fling yourself into the light.
Dark was just a dream.

52

My darling, let go.
Anything you hold onto
will bite you in the end.

53

Throw out your used clothes
and put on new ones. That is
the story of death.

54

Like a lost ghost, the
lonely mind still thinks of fear
and loathing as real.

55

Come out from your cave,
become a cosmic angel:
consecrate someone.

56

We are gods thrown back
to earth to learn the folly
of flesh and desire.

57

Have the courage to
say – at the end of the day –
I will try again.

58

A new day. Life will
be as easy or as hard
as we think it is.

59

Every cry ~ a new
life. Every breath ~ a prelude
waiting to be played.

60

Desire, when fulfilled,
creates another. Candy
becomes compulsive.

61

Life is like a deep,
flowing river. Swim with the
flow, not against it.

62

We are not living
our lives. We are being lived
by the Creator.

63

How do people feel
when they're with you? That will be
your true legacy.

64

The cow eats grass and
laps up gruel. From her sweet milk
is Shanti sustained.

Three

Suffering

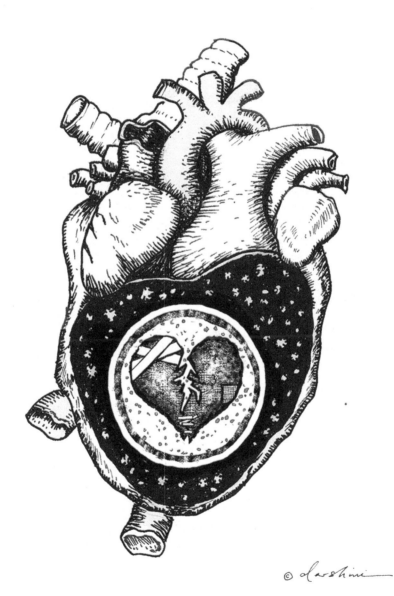

65

Rain, waves, hurricanes,
storms and sleet sweep through the cracks
of our unhealed hearts.

66

Through struggle we find
our way to grace, and through grace
we find our way home.

67

Only gratitude
will keep the black dog at bay
busy with its bone.

68

Peace to all beings.
May they have kindness. May they
have freedom from pain.

69

Accept life's sadness,
then stretch like cats in the sun
when night is over.

70

Judgment causes pain.
Only understanding will
give us peace of mind.

71

Pull your weeds of woe.
Water your sad heart with love.
Let your suffering go.

72

The mind's habit is
to sell us on the belief
that we must suffer.

73

When we've forgotten
that we are part of God's play,
suffering returns.

74

When pain returns, the
student prepares her notebook
for the next lesson.

75

The miracle of
surrender can transform your
suffering to peace.

76

We subdue our pain
by loving the sorry beast
into submission.

77

We weave light and dark.
We shadow dance. In time we
forget to suffer.

78

Your pain bears its own
cure. Look inside for that light
in a lump of coal.

79

Unhappiness is
a barrier to our self
realization.

80

Birth. Squall. Disorder.
Misery. Pot holes. Trouble.
And then the page turns.

81

Aligning ourselves
with now, suffering ends and
balance is restored

82

I am the postman
for impassioned pleas that all
find freedom from pain.

83

Take your suffering.
Toss it on the bonfire of
love. Toast marshmallows.

84

I am no longer
who I used to be. Sorrow
has lost its appeal.

85

When you have released
attachment to suffering
baby's breath will bloom.

86

We need suffering
until we learn it's lessons.
Then it takes it's leave.

87

Tell me about your
despair and I will tell you
mine. We'll feel better.

88

Do not run from grief,
find remedies in the pain.
Diamonds come from stones.

Four

Ego

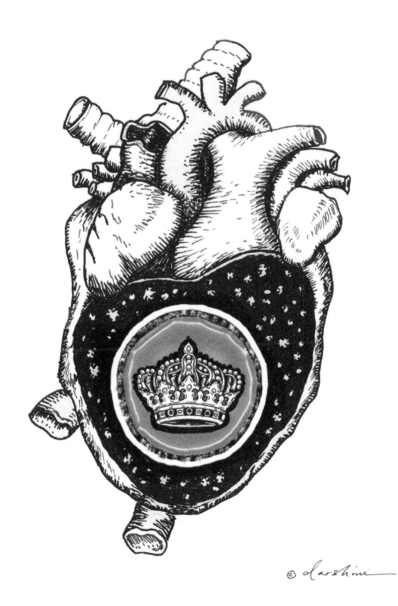

89

Ego is my dense
and foolish teacher. My best
friend is gratitude

90
Crazy how we cling
to our chains. Why are we so
afraid of freedom?

91

The unseen is the
basis of the seen, just as
breath sustains our life.

92

Not being without
fault myself, I should not look
for fault in others.

93

We are addicted
to our stories. Let's ask who
we are without them.

94

When we feel the joy
of the miraculous, we
know we have come home.

95

Today will never
happen again. Tomorrow
does not exist.

96

Our bloated egos
are blind to our true beauty
and pure perfection.

97

Inquire wisely
into personality,
then watch it dissolve.

98

Winning does not tempt
me. Being defeated is
how I grow stronger.

99

When we have lost all
sense of a personal self
we become the Self.

100

I see Light through
a crack in my ego. Break me
open; set me free.

101
When you talk, you are
only repeating what you
know. Try listening.

102

Without internal
innocence, this morning's bath
will not clean you up.

103

Wanting others to
be happy brings joy. Grasping
it for ourselves - grief.

104

We see what we think
and feel; hardly ever what
is in front of us.

105

Our choice is to feed
the ego or remember
that we are Spirit.

106

Egotism stalks
the world, breeding greed, while love
creates contentment.

107

Give up false ideas
and your quest for true ideas.
They do not exist.

108

Expectation means
being frustrated by God's
perfect authorship

109

She is brave who can
claim the hardest victory
over self-conceit.

110

Manage the ego
and cultivate the heart. This
is the way to God.

111

Just accept yourself.
Defensiveness is warfare
waged against spirit.

112

Die to the self and
birth to the One. Heaven will
ravish you with song.

113

If we remembered
how powerful our thoughts are,
we'd think more carefully.

114

Free will means choosing
your attitude in any
life situation.

115

One choice is to feed
the ego. The other is
to starve it to death.

116

When my ego has
had its day, I will glisten
like a god in love.

117

Why do I react?
I cannot change others but
I can change myself.

118

The I behind the
eye can't be seen. It's a dream:
a thought gone amuck.

119

Unwilling to see
our own faults, we are experts
at seeing others'.

Five

Spiritual Practice

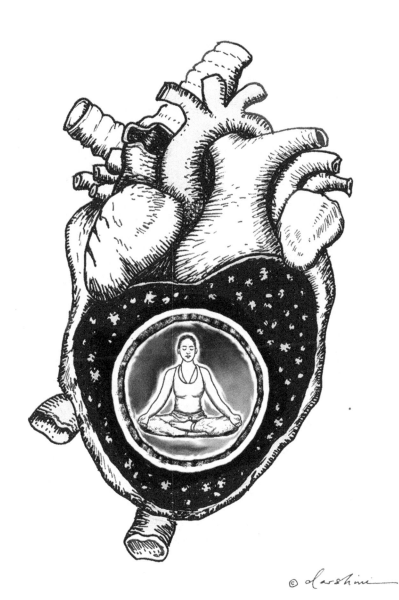

© Darshini

120

Breathing in is grace.
Breathing out is surrender.
In between is peace.

121

Silence is behind
every thought and sensation.
Seek it and rest there.

122

Our moments of true
surrender are miracles
of self-mastery.

123

Surround yourself with
people who treat you well. Pray
for the ones who don't.

124

If we neglect being
kind now, there may come a time
we find it's too late.

125

Make life simple: trust
in the universe and keep
kindness in your heart.

126

Sometimes when we are
kind in small and simple ways
a life can be changed.

127

Everyone is my
teacher. Let me gain wisdom from
every one I meet.

128

Life is a movie
whose end has already been
written in the wind.

129

Our only bondage
is in not seeing that we
are actually free.

130

The voice of wisdom
can only be heard when our
mind and tongue are still.

131

Let me see God's Light
even if it blasts me off
the face of the earth.

132

If we don't connect
with our inner wisdom, our
lives are just drama.

133

Learn to act and think
with love. Then be of service
to all breathing beings

134

We're here to hold out
our hand to others when they
need a little help.

135

Help as lovingly
as possible. Give thanks you
are able to serve.

136

Service may or may
not help others, but it will
certainly help you.

137

Use your obstacles
as the raw materials
for a work of art.

138

Every breath we take
through the heart can help
heal all sentient beings.

139

Let the foundation
of your spiritual practice
be altruism.

140

Between light and dark
we can make a choice. Let's choose
illumination.

141

Service to others
and reverence for all life
will guide us to Truth.

142

The end result of
our spiritual practice will
be infinite love.

143

Meditation is
when we quiet our thinking
and temper our tongue.

144

If you feel alone
practice loving kindness and
you will receive it.

145

I am not the doer.
Nor are you. So who are we
to forgive? For what?

146

To get to bliss, pass
need for approval, need to
control, need to judge.

147

The strawberry plucked
while trapped between two tigers
is always sweetest.

148

Dancing with my soul
the music I move to is
exquisite and true.

149

The highest form of
happiness is compassion
for all live beings.

150

In accepting my
non-peace, I find peace in the
act of surrender.

151

All things happen as
they are supposed to happen.
It is Cosmic Law.

152

My prayer of solace
Is for you. Will you take it
and pass it along?

153

Have a perfect day
by seeing the perfection
in it as it is.

Six

Whimsy

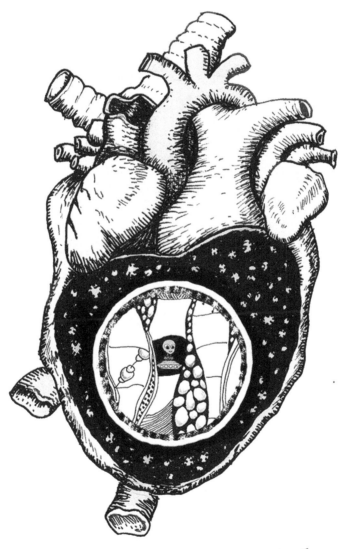

154

I am grateful for
my gratitude. Without it
I would be a toad.

155

Why muck about in
the gloom when there is always
a light in the dark.

156

The instinct of a
dog is often better than
the reason of man.

157

I forgot to light
my third eye today. Alas,
I am in the dark.

158

When we dance with the
shadows of who we think we
are, we're bound to trip.

159

He had no smile so
I gave him mine. Then we both
smiled and were happy.

160

I've finished my coke
and my popcorn. The dream on
the screen will soon end.

161

Can't get to heaven
in dancing shoes, but happy
hearts can waltz us there.

162

Plump lips and hips are
weird reminders of kisses
and decay. That's life.

163

My body is a
wonder. Decay has set in.
Still it wants to waltz.

164

Don't just sniff at life,
gobble it up with gusto.
Dogs will show you how.

165

The whole world is a
madhouse. Some are mad for wealth.
I am mad for Love.

166

Splendid nightmare, keep
your horrors happy, because when
morning comes you die.

167

Who are we without
our stories? Impeccable light
and kick ass angels.

168

My haiku bubble
out of me like belches from
A savory meal.

169

I reek with longing.
I starve. I want to gobble
God up for dinner.

170
You are free from sin.
Flush the toilet and begin
again. Poems await.

171

A new haiku for
a new day. May it be one
of piffle and play!

172
You are good enough.
Drink more water and dare to
be ordinary.

173

Flitting about on
a self-important stage, my
ego starts to stink.

174

Living inside a
junker of failing flesh, I'm
happy it still runs.

175

Light coming after
night can devour your woes
in a single gulp.

176

Dear Spirit, be with
me. Become my google guide
to the promised land.

Seven

Transformation

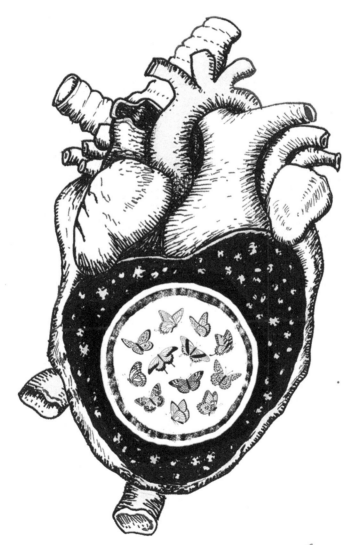

177

Aum is the echo
of the hills, the rustle of
leaves, the air we breathe.

178

You are in the Light,
the Light is in you and your
essence is the Light.

179

Smile when you want a
smile from another. Give when
your cupboard is bare.

180

Grumbling about my
unsatisfactory day.
A rose pedal drops.

181

Opening our heart
to the sacredness of life
replenishes us.

182

When we understand
that everything is nothing
we will become free.

183

Not only can we
find ourselves, we can also
choose to free ourselves.

184

From myopic self-
absorption to freedom, we
determine our lives.

185

Merging with skylight,
each moment is a chance to
spread our wings and fly.

186

If we want freedom,
everything we do must be
an act of worship.

187

My birthday is a
happy day. I am one year
closer to going home.

188

Between the lines there
are spaces. Although empty,
they hold everything

189

Accept this moment
and feel its sweet spaciousness
dissolve your constraints.

190

If prayers can't alter
what has been preordained, then
'thank you' becomes prayer.

191

You are sublimely
pure. You are free. Remove your
disguise and dazzle.

192

I am free when I
remember I am being lived
through and need nothing.

193

Each bag of bones stands
alone, a breath away from
rubble and rebirth.

194

There is no freedom
from the human condition,
only from our lies.

195

Our torn places make
us beautiful when they are
mended with prayer.

196

Death is not an end.
It is a transformation;
a portal to Source.

197

Lord, I know you will
transfigure me if only
I open my heart.

198

When we believe in
good and bad, our lives reflect
the resulting stress

199

Nothing has power
except that which you give it.
You, alone, decide.

200

Release the endless
loop of your story. There is
no then, only now.

201

Reactions consigned
to a compost heap become
rich fodder for growth.

202

Hell is insistence
on my own way forever.
Total disaster.

203

Our well-being does
not depend on how we feel
but how we accept.

204

When we blame others
we only hurt ourselves through
self-comdemnation.

205

You are a diamond:
a lump of coal that has done
well under pressure.

206

True healing begins
By embracing everything
exactly as is.

207

There is no sin, just
ignorance; no darkness, just
the absence of light.

208

A pure, white light
is surrounding you. Take a
step inside. Ignite.

209

Make life simple: trust
in the universe and keep
kindness in your heart.

210

Between light and dark
we can make a choice. Let's choose
illumination.

211

Sunburst in the sky.
All souls turn their faces to
the living light.

212

A small kindness can
change someone's life forever
Let's be lavish.

213

In some ways we're all
wounded animals. We must
care for each other

214

My gift of solace
is for you. Will you take it
and pass it along?

215

No one needs your smile
as much as someone who doesn't
have one of their own.

216

There is always light.
It's there to be found, it just
takes an open heart.

217

Gratitude is not
just for the feel good, but the
feel bad of life, too.

218
Finding peace within
means settling ourselves into
pure self acceptance.

Eight

Spirit/God

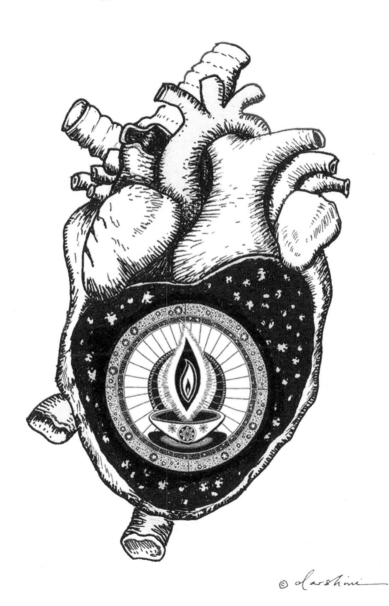

219

Bed in the landscape,
shooting stars for a night light.
Time to dream of God.

220

Everything we crave
will come back and bite us.
Safest to crave God.

221

Facilitate your
birth. Intercourse with God is
the warm up to bliss.

222

This universe is
the beautiful body of
an excellent God.

223

We are not this flesh.
We are not this mind. We are
but Spirit dreaming.

224

We can always turn
adversity into love.
by following Source.

225

Look into the eyes
of thieves and flies, cows and clerks,
and you will find God.

226

Keep quiet. Don't think.
Do not doubt your majesty.
You are one with One.

227

At your core is Soul;
virgin, pure and egoless.
Look there for your truth.

228

Water must return
to the river, as our self
must return to Source.

229

I am running out of
time. Let me use it well in
clamoring after God.

230

I am only as
distant from God as I feel.
And only as near.

231

God becomes the clay
from which we and our trinkets
are manufactured.

232

Wherever you see
beauty manifested, you
see the Beloved.

233

When we've forgotten
that we are part of God's play,
suffering returns.

234

I am barely born.
I know nothing. Spirit, teach
me Your alphabet.

235

When everything is
dedicated to the One,
life becomes sacred.

236

Nothing we feel is
wrong. All we need to do is
give it to Spirit.

237

Love of the whole is
love of the parts. We can't love
God and not the thief.

238

I am not this flesh,
this breath, this death. Beyond it
I am the "I Am."

239

Stuff will never be
enough. Only Spirit can
ever fill us up.

240

Switching on the light
in our hearts illuminates
the divine within.

241

Let's hold hands and touch
lips. Let's climb the ladder to
nirvana and bliss.

242

Every day we breathe
in the out breath of God
we become more real.

243

Soft overcomes hard,
gentle overcomes rigid.
That is spirit's way.

244

Every hour is a
miracle. Every day is
a thought form of God.

245

Silence is your source.
Om shanti shanti shanti.
Return to Silence.

Nine

Love

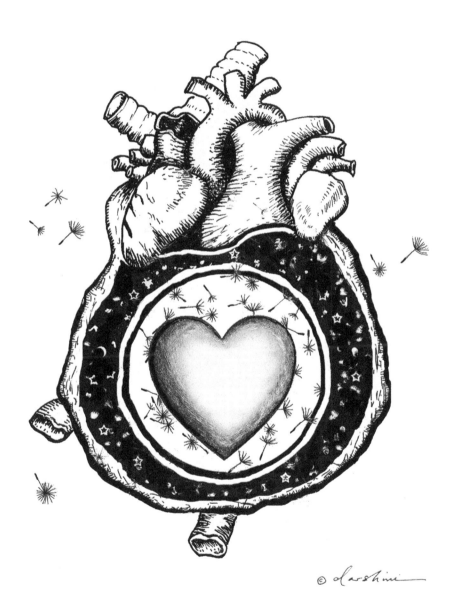

246

If Grace allows us
love, who can challenge our choice
of life companions?

247

Peace, patience and love
can be revived whenever
we open our hearts

248

Aligning our life
with love, the companionship
of angels is ours.

249

Love is our true wealth.
It will never lose it's worth
in the stock market.

250

Seen through the eyes of
love, all beings are beautiful
and at one with God.

251

Extend to yourself
unconditional love. Then
you can love others.

252

A true search for God
begins, continues and ends
with unselfish love.

253

Love is the only
solution to the problems
of our existence.

254

Why are we here on
earth for this short stay, if not
to learn how to love?

255

Every action is
either an action of love
or a call for love.

256

I empty my mind
of rocks and stones so it can
carry compassion

257

I want a world where
no child weeps and love flows through
veins like liquid light.

258

True love is perfect,
pure and impartial. This is
who we really are.

259

Every act of love
raises the vibration of
the whole universe.

260

The more I love, the
more my love flows until I
touch eternity.

261

I will touch heaven
when love snuffs out the curse
of intolerance.

262

Love for love's sake
alone is the highest form
of recreation.

263

Why are we here on
earth for this short stay if not
to learn how to love?

264

Love is the only
answer to any problem
we may encounter.

265

Dogs, with their fervent
love, are the role model I
use for how to live.

266

Unlock the door of
your caged heart. There is more to
life than feeling safe.

267

Come out of your cave.
Become an open, sharing
heart and love someone.
(Anyone. Everyone.)

268

Tell me, what makes song?
I think it's when we reach out
with love to someone.

269

Thinking creates time.
Past and future are just thoughts.
Love is eternal.

270

Issue a permit
for universal love and
give it right of way.

271

Loving each other
is the end for which all else
is preparation.

272

May our lives become
one with the ocean of love
that lives within us.

273

It's the way it is:
searing pain, piercing heartbreak.
But still we can love.

274

True divinity
is found in formlessness:
no face, only Love.

275

Look within and find
what never changes: It's the
love that brought you here.

276

Learn to think and act
with love. Then be of service
to all breathing beings.

277

I am running out of
time. Spirit – awaken me.
Let me die of love.

278

Love is the highest
vibration there is. Climb that
ladder in your soul.

279

Making love with the
origin of life unlocks
the door to your Self.

280

Why let fear stand in
the way of love? It is time
to rewire your life.

281

Awaken with each
breath. Love with every beat of
your infinite heart.

Acknowledgments

With heartfelt thanks to Allanya Guenther, Melanie Prema Eaton, and Frank Sanje Elliot for their proof reading, suggestions, insights, opinions and encouragements. And thanks to Adriane Shanti Burkhart, Mary Guenther, Jerri-Jo Idarius, Sheryl Christmas, Lily Komalta Helmer, Louisa Gonyou, Janette Leclerc-Law, Alexandra Richardson and Renee Beck for their acceptance and appreciation of—I was going to say "my" work. But anything good I have ever been given is not for me to claim credit. It is only for me to gratefully share.

No one is luckier than I for the family and friends I am honored to have. I love them all to the moon and back.

About the Author

Skyler Darshini Freimann is a retired mental health care practitioner, poet and award-winning photographer. She is the author of "Ring of Dreams," a photographic Passion Play using her photographs of professional boxers along with Biblical quotes, and "One With The Sofa, a Taoist Guide for the Physically Challenged, a book of her art along with Taoist inspired spiritual teachings. Her books can be found on www.amazon.com. She is also featured on her mandala art website "Darshini Arts," an online business featuring her mandala T-shirts and greeting cards. (www.darshiniarts.com)

An adherent of Advaita Vedanta, the Hindu path of non-dualism, Skyler's Hindu spiritual name is "Darshini" which means "bringer of light." All of her art contains a commitment to shining light on the many paths to healing that so many of us undertake. She is a lifelong student, practitioner and teacher of spiritual traditions and lives in the Pacific Northwest with her beloved human and animal family. Although disabled and chronically ill for many years, she treasures life and hopes to remain an active artist, student of life, seeker and lover of all beings until she moves on.

Made in the USA
Las Vegas, NV
19 September 2021